City

Animals

Contents

Hello fellow aliens! What do you want to know about planet Earth?

City

Animals

Hiya, I'm Zeek.

Hi, I'm Finn.

91120000418725

Calling all aliens!

Are you planning a holiday to planet Earth?

Finn and Zeek are here to help.

'City Animals'

Published by MAVERICK ARTS PUBLISHING LTD

Studio 11, City Business Centre, 6 Brighton Road,

Horsham, West Sussex, RH13 5BB, +44 (0)1403 256941

© Maverick Arts Publishing Limited August 2019

A CIP catalogue record for this book is available at the British Library.

ISBN 978-1-84886-478-8

Maverick publishing
www.maverickbooks.co.uk

Credits:
Finn & Zeek illustrations by Jake McDonald, Bright Illustration Agency
Cover: Jake McDonald/Bright, Wild Wonders of Europe/Geslin/naturepl.com
Inside: **Naturepl.com:** Cyril Ruoso/Minden (6, 20 & 30), Nayan Khanolkar (8, 14 & 31),
Laurent Geslin (10, 12 & 30), Sam Hobson (11 & 30), Martin Gabriel (16 & 31), Aflo (17 & 31), Florian Möllers (18, 19 & 30), Cyril Ruoso (21), Shattil & Rozinski (22, 23 & 30), Steven Kazlowski (24 & 30). Shutterstock: DMstudio House (27 & 31).

Turquoise

This book is rated as: Turquoise Band (Guided Reading)

INCOMING MESSAGE

Dear Finn and Zeek,

We want to visit Earth. We're hoping to visit some cities but want to see animals as well.

Can you tell us about some of the animals that live in cities?

From
Tik and Tok
(Planet Sit-ee)

Many types of animals live in human cities! One reason is that cities are getting larger. As cities grow, they take over space where animals used to live. So animals have had to start living in the cities too.

Let's take a closer look at some of these city animals!

Living in the City

Animals that live in the city have lots of problems.

★ They can't move around as freely as they would in the countryside.

★ They may not be able to get the food they normally eat.

★ They may be in danger from traffic.

★ Some animals get ill because of **pollution**.

★ They may not get along well with humans.

But there are some good things about living in the city.

★ Animals can eat food left behind by humans.

★ Animals living in cities may not be hunted so much by **predators**.

Pigeons live everywhere in cities! The city is a good place for pigeons, because there are lots of tall buildings. Pigeons build their nests on the tall buildings.

Peregrine Falcons

Peregrine falcons are hunting birds. They like to hunt smaller birds like pigeons. So when pigeons moved to the city, peregrine falcons moved there too.

Clever Creatures Foxes

Foxes have been living in cities for at least fifty years!

In fact, there are often more foxes in the city than in the countryside.

Foxes like living in the city because there is lots of food for them to eat – from bugs to rats to human rubbish. Foxes are clever, so they have quickly learnt how to deal with the dangers of the city.

In 2011, there was a fox living on the 72nd floor of the Shard in London!

In the big city of Mumbai in India, you might see leopards! Leopards live alongside people in this big city. The city is a good place for the leopards because there are lots of wild dogs. Leopards hunt and eat the wild dogs.

The wild dogs are dangerous for people because they have **diseases** - so the leopards are helping people by hunting the dogs!

House Geckos

House geckos live in Southeast Asia.
You can tell from their name that house
geckos live in houses!

They like to live on house walls. The lights
in the houses **attract** bugs – and the
geckos eat the bugs!

The biggest city in Japan is Tokyo. Lots of animals have moved to live in Tokyo.

One of these is the tanuki (called a 'racoon dog' in English). Some tanuki even live in the grounds of the Imperial Palace!

Wild boar have moved into German towns and cities. They usually come to the city in the winter months when they are looking for food. Wild boar are shy, but they dig up the green parts of the city. They also leave big piles of mud. This is quite annoying for the people who live in the city.

How can something so cute do so much damage?

Boars dig up the grass because they are looking for food. They don't eat rubbish – they like eating acorns!

Sometimes animals and humans don't mix very well. Chacma baboons cause lots of trouble in Cape Town, South Africa. They often break into houses, take over restaurants and even steal food right out of people's hands!

Uh oh...

21

Black bears have moved into some cities in North America. They like eating rubbish from people's bins.

Bears are very clever. They know they will find food where humans live. They sometimes break into cars and houses to steal food.

Have you got any chips?

Polar Bears

Polar bears are shy, and they don't want to live in cities. But because the **polar ice caps** have been melting, some polar bears have had to move to the city to find food.

Hungry polar bears are dangerous to humans. So humans are trying to move polar bears back to safer places, away from cities.

MESSAGE SENT

Dear Tik and Tok,

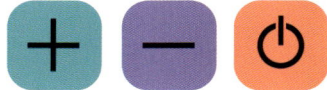

Cities can be scary places for animals. But some animals like city life! Humans are helping some animals to find new homes, outside the city.

If you are visiting Japan, be sure to visit the sika deer in Nara. They live in the city and can be fed special deer snacks!

From,
Finn and Zeek x

Sika deer, Japan

Quiz

1. Which of these is not so much of a danger for animals in cities?
a) Pollution
b) Traffic
c) Being hunted by predators

2. Where can you find city leopards?
a) Mumbai, India
b) London, UK
c) Tokyo, Japan

3. What is a tanuki called in English?
a) Fox dog
b) Raccoon dog
c) Dog bear

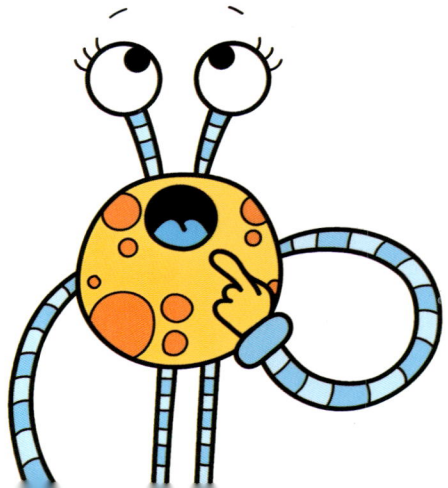

4. What do the city boars eat?

a) Acorns

b) Rubbish

c) Cars

5. Which of these animals doesn't mix well with humans?

a) House geckos

b) Pigeons

c) Chacma baboons

5. Polar bears go into cities for food because...

a) They want to eat from bins

b) They like the lights

c) The ice caps are melting and they have to find food somewhere else

Index/Glossary

Attract pg 16
To feel a pull towards something.

Disease pg 15
An illness that hurts a person, animal or plant.

Canada

U.K.

Germany

U.S.A.

South
Africa

Polar ice caps pg 24, 29

Big areas of ice at the north and south poles.

Pollution pg 8, 28

Harmful waste that can hurt the environment.

Predator pg 9, 28

An animal that hunts other animals (prey).

Japan

India

Southeast
Asia

Book Bands for Guided Reading

The Institute of Education book banding system is a scale of colours that reflects the various levels of reading difficulty. The bands are assigned by taking into account the content, the language style, the layout and phonics. Word, phrase and sentence level work is also taken into consideration.

Maverick Early Readers are a bright, attractive range of books covering the pink to white bands. All of these books have been book banded for guided reading to the industry standard and edited by a leading educational consultant.

Pink
Red
Yellow
Blue
Green
Orange
Turquoise
Purple
Gold
White

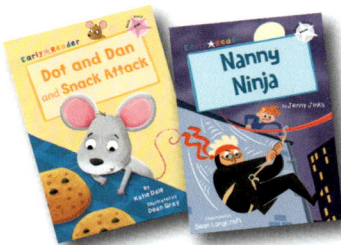

Fiction

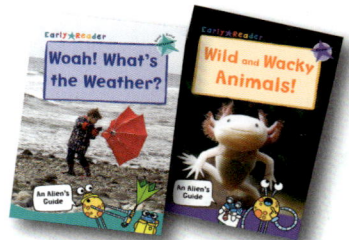

Non-fiction

To view the whole Maverick Readers scheme, visit our website at www.maverickearlyreaders.com

Or scan the QR code above to view our scheme instantly!